50 EASY CONTEMPORARY PIECES FOR FINGERSTYLE GUITAR

GILBERT ISBIN

To access the online audio recording go to:
WWW.MELBAY.COM/31004MEB

WWW.MELBAY.COM

Contents

Foreword

This collection of 50 original easy pieces was composed for classical and fingerstyle guitarists of all ages.

The compositions are written entirely in first and second position. All pieces are enjoyable and acessible with singable melodies, easy colorful chords with lots of open strings, and creative chord progressions.

The tempo suggestions are optional. They are left to the players as a matter of personal interpretation. The fingerings are optional too. Feel free to experiment and find your own practical fingerings for the fretting hand.

Some of the compositions refer to world music (Raga 1 and 2) or to the blues (*Moon Gazing Blues, Blue Tale,....*). Others are slightly influenced by jazz (*Better Together than Alone, September Reflection*), or polyphonic music (*A Peaceful Place, A Clear Path, A Brief Encounter,...*)

The note values and rhythms were intentionally kept simple. Standard notation is included, but each piece is also presented in tablature which makes it easy to visualise strings, frets and fingers to use. For ease of learning, I've included recordings of all the pieces.

Gilbert Isbin

About the Author

Gilbert Isbin

Belgian guitarist Gilbert Isbin is one of the most interesting, dynamic and poetic composers writing for the guitar today.

Isbin's compositional and performing style defies genre, blending elements of contemporary classical, jazz, early music, world music and improvisation. In favorable comparisons with the likes of Ralph Towner and Egberto Gismonti, his music has been described as "oblique, subtle, and hauntingly beautiful."

He has composed more than 400 pieces for guitar(s), lute(s) and small ensembles and performed in festivals and major venues throughout Europe and the US.

As a leader and co-leader, he has released an impressive string of recordings on various labels with such international acclaimed artists as Cameron Brown, Joe Fonda, Bruce Arnold, Jeff Gauthier, Scott Walton, Hugh Hopper and Sandro di Stefano.

In a Subtle Way

Gilbert Isbin

A Clear Path
2
♩ = 66
Gilbert Isbin
To Coda

17

21

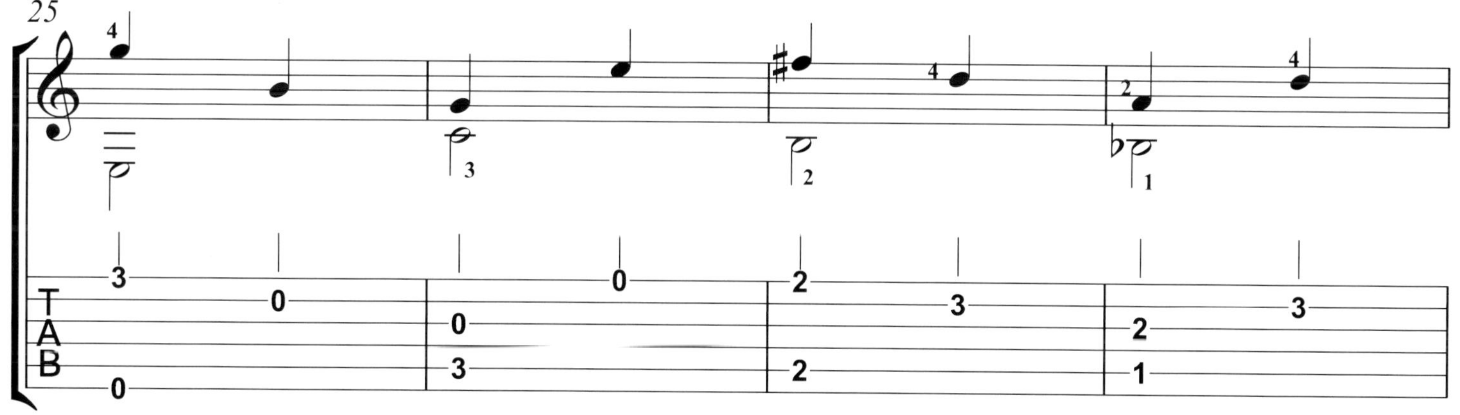
25

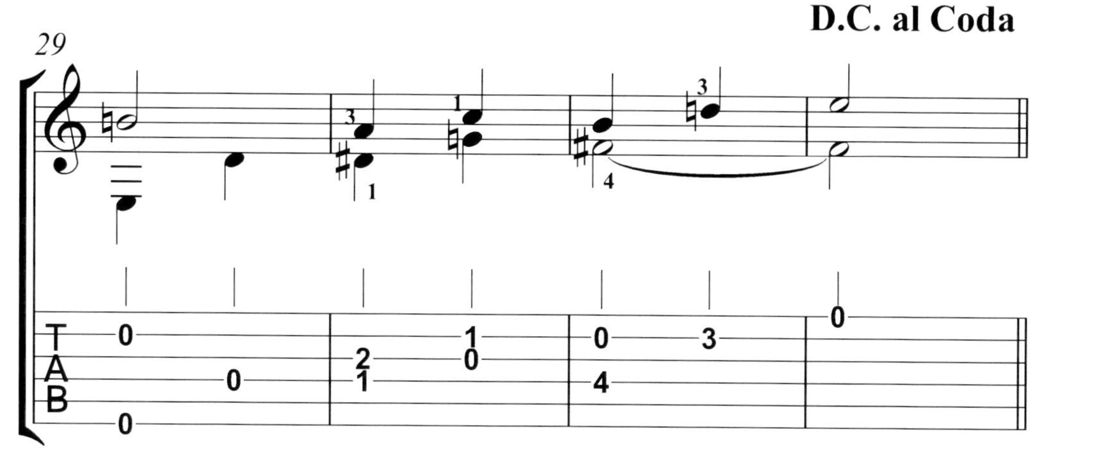
D.C. al Coda
29

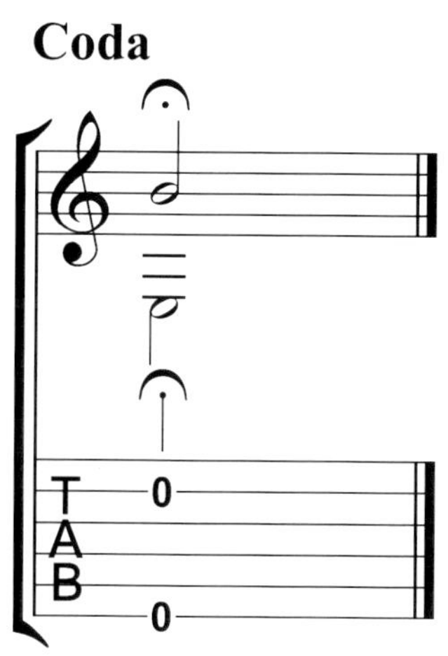
Coda

A Peaceful Place

Gilbert Isbin

21
TAB
26
TAB
30
1.
TAB
34
2.
TAB

Away From You

To Coda
D.C. al Coda
Coda

5
Stay Here
♩ = 74
Gilbert Isbin

Blue Tale
6
♩ = 72
Gilbert Isbin
rit.

Because I Asked

Sweet Love

Come Away with Me

Gilbert Isbin

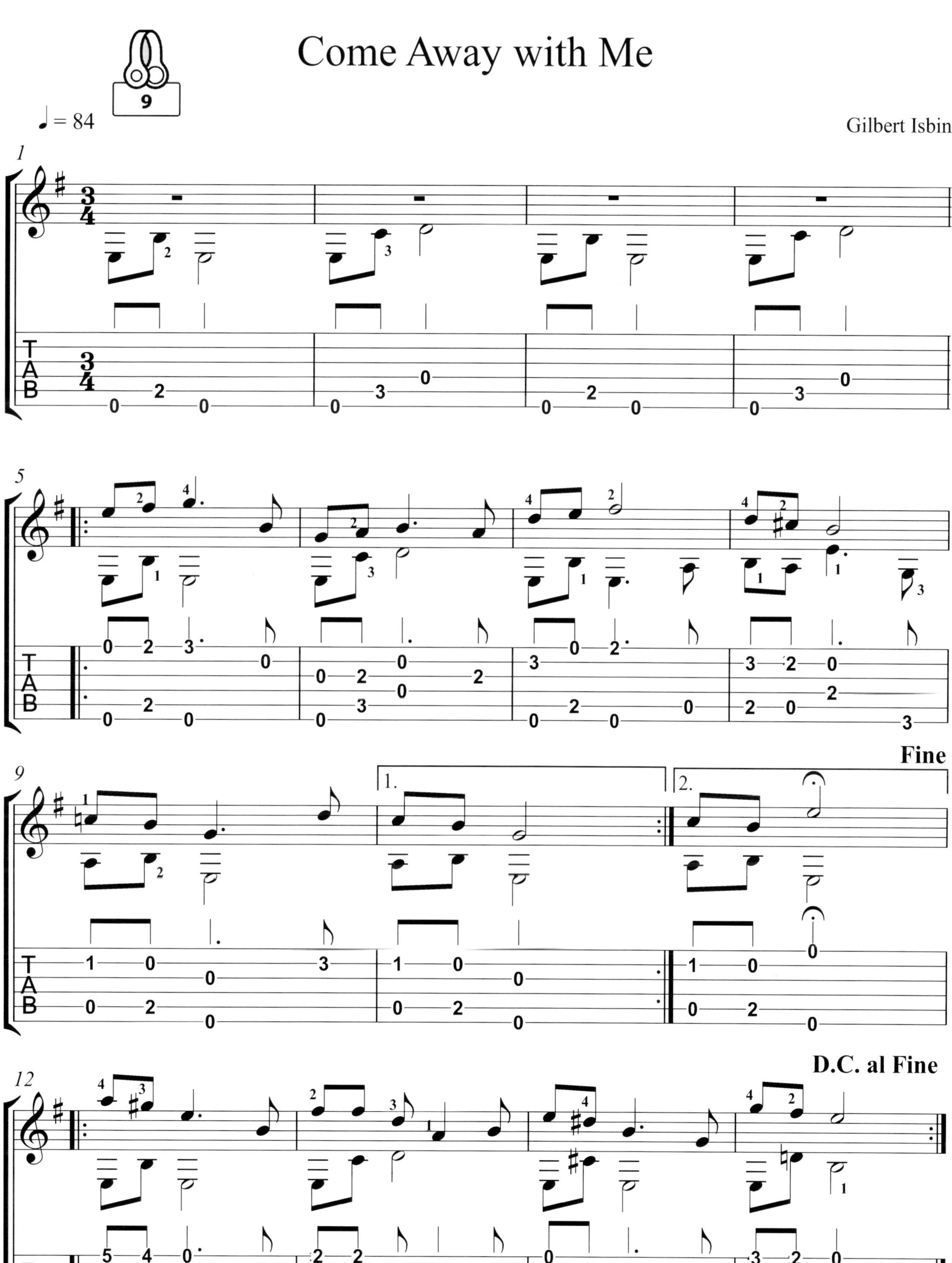

Raga #1
10
♩ = 72
Gilbert Isbin
Fine
D.C. al Fine

A Time For Two

Canson

Life Finds a Way

Gilbert Isbin

Playful

Gilbert Isbin

Better Together than Alone

Gilbert Isbin

16
D.C. al Fine
20
1.
2.

Moon Gazing Blues

Gilbert Isbin

Letter

18
Dream On
♩ = 72
Gilbert Isbin
1.

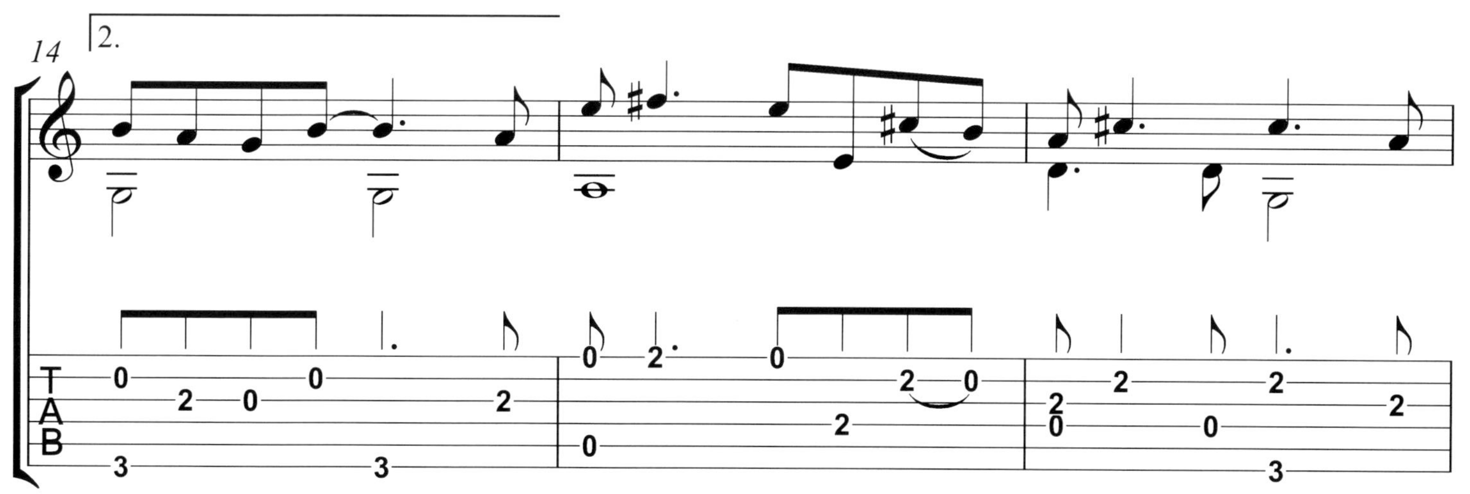

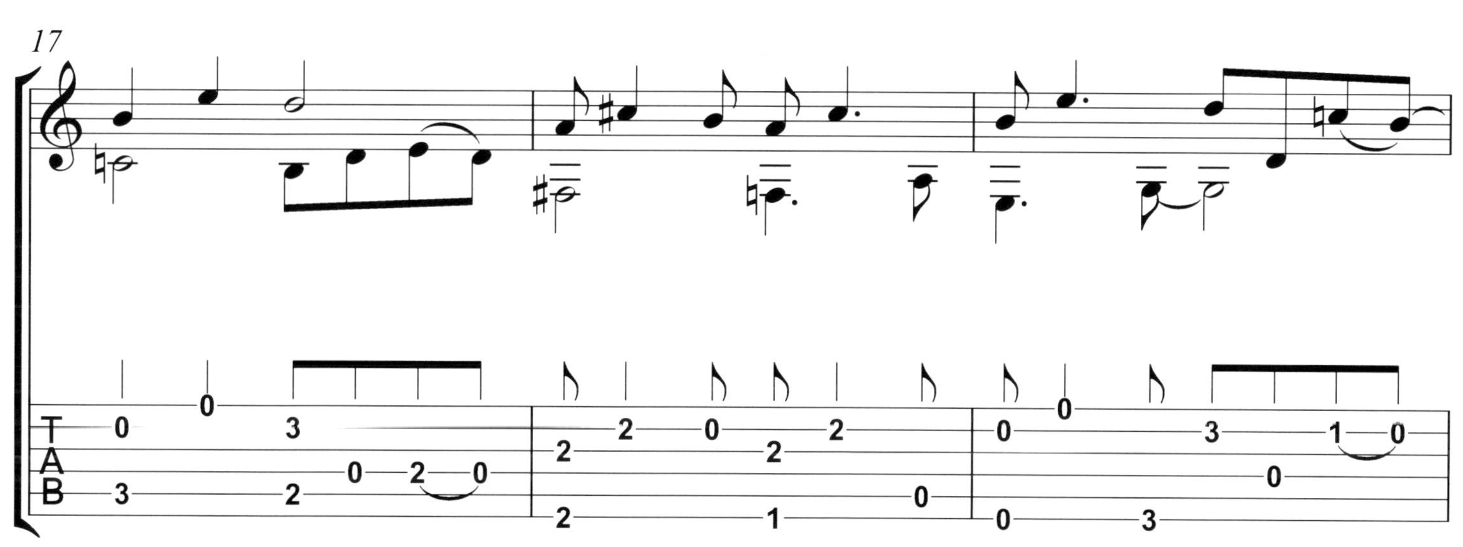

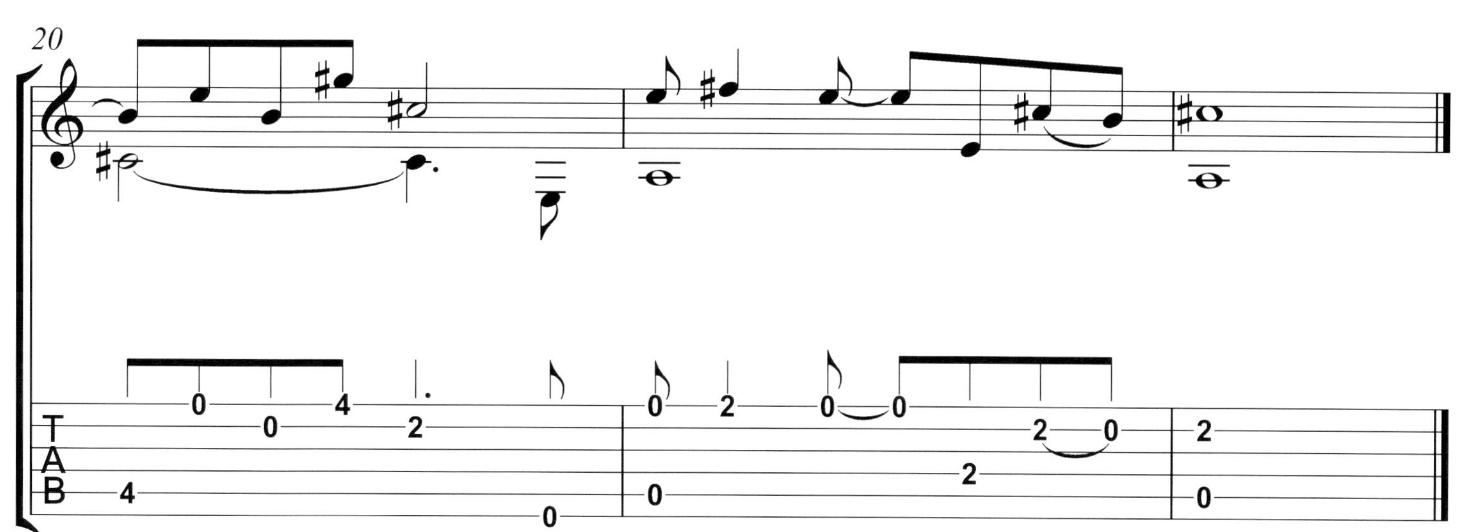

One Day

A Brief Encounter

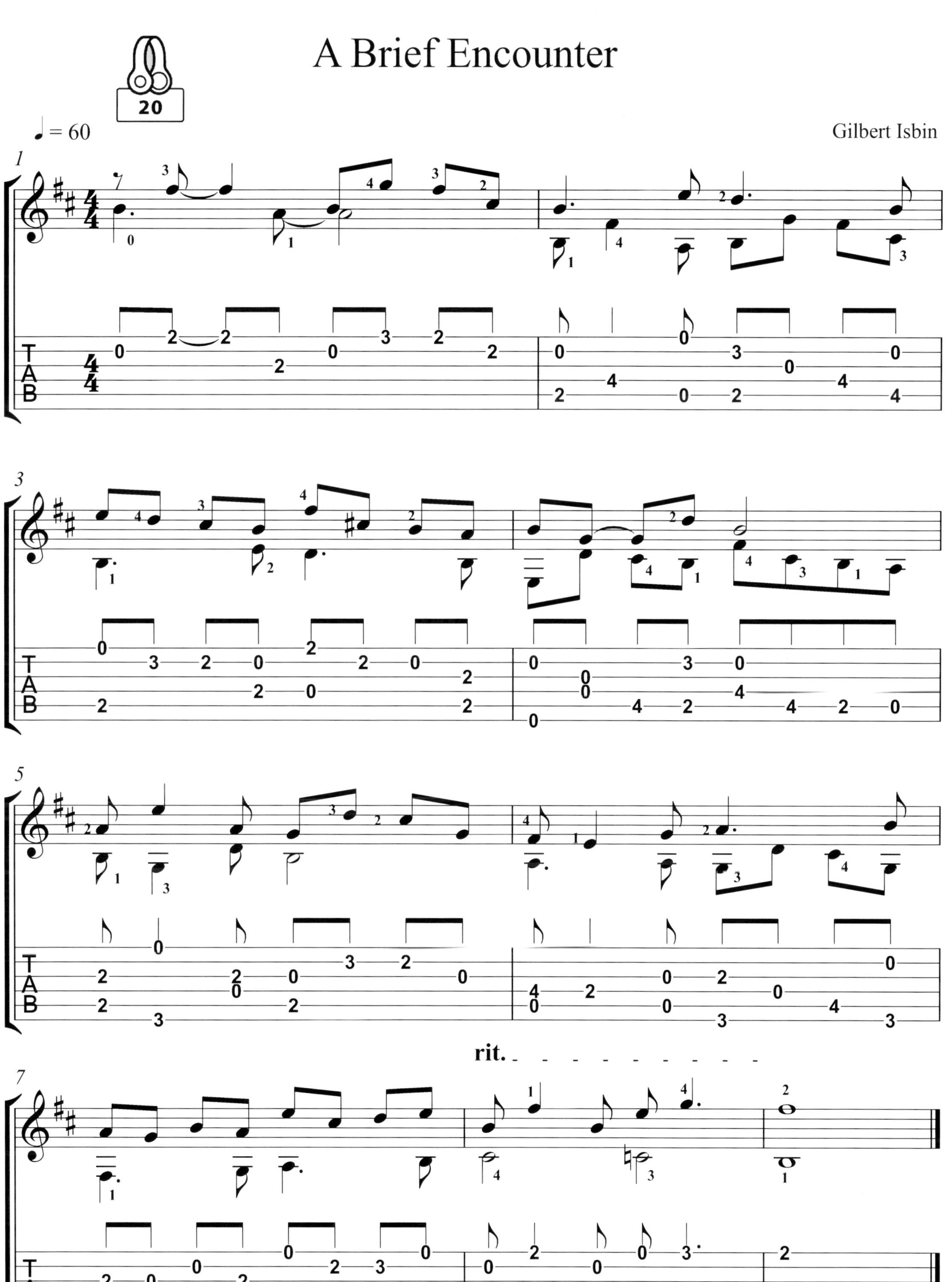

September Reflection

D.C. al Coda **Coda**

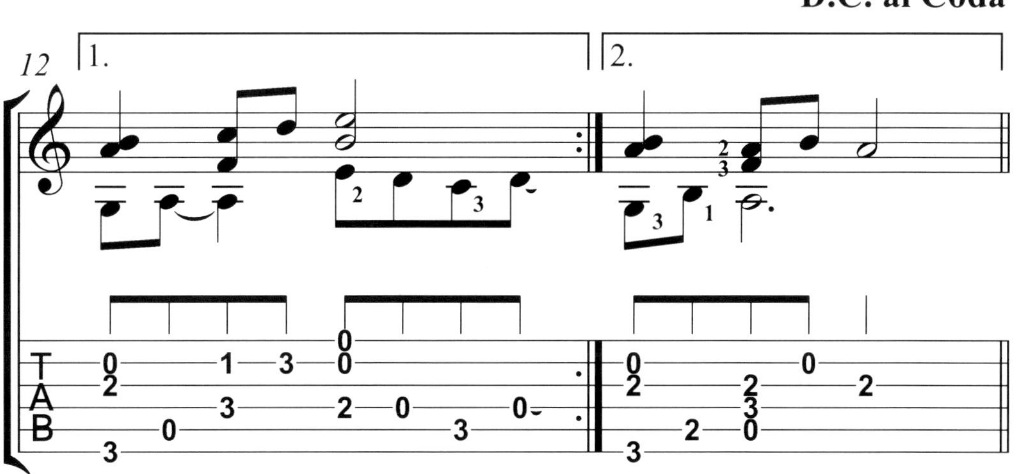

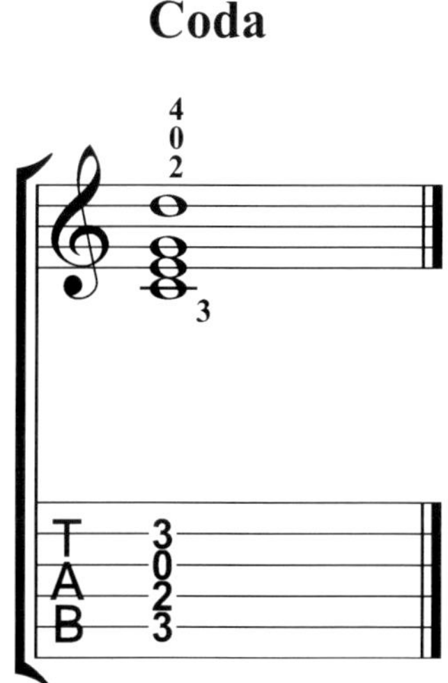

Happy Meeting

Gilbert Isbin

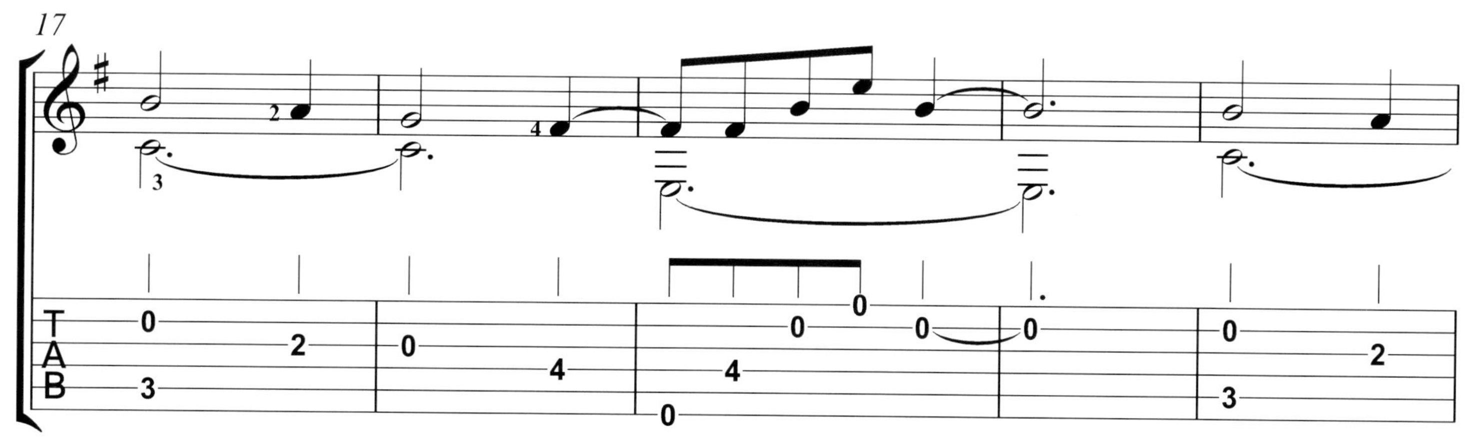
17
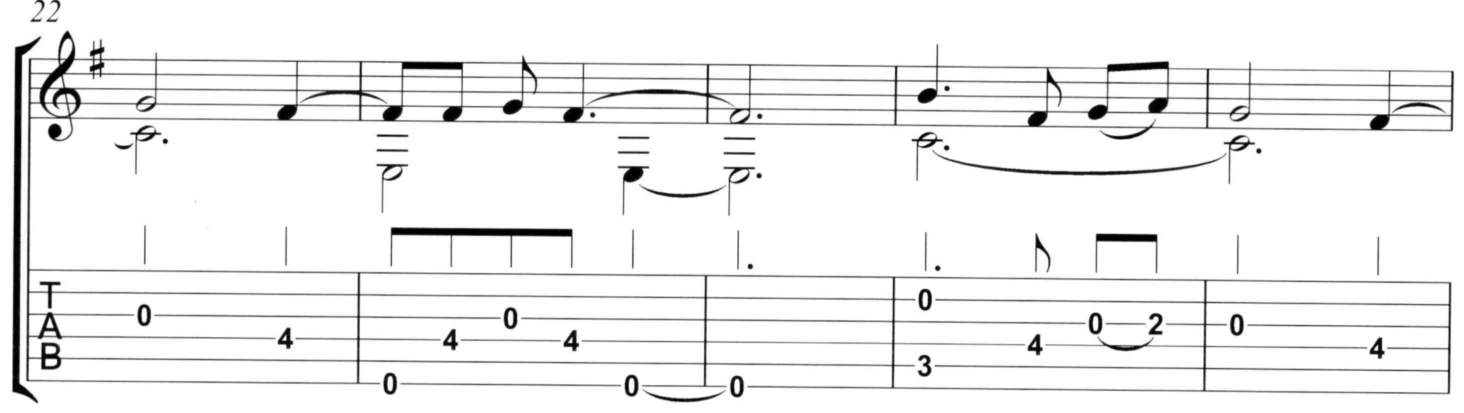
22
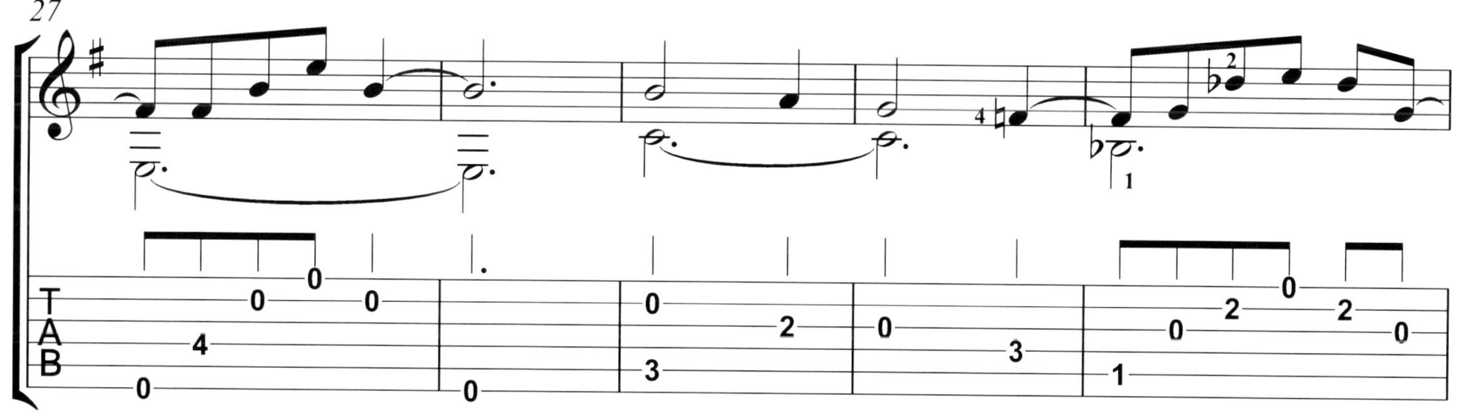
27

32
D.C. al Coda
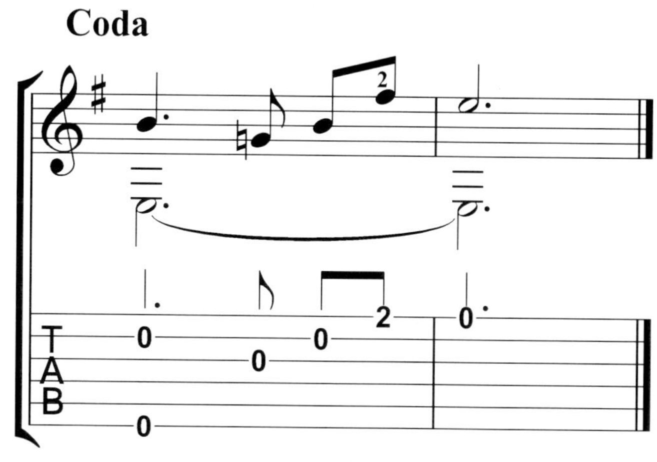
Coda

It's Funny

Gilbert Isbin

14
T
A
B
D.C. al Fine
1.
2.
17

Into Heaven

Gilbert Isbin

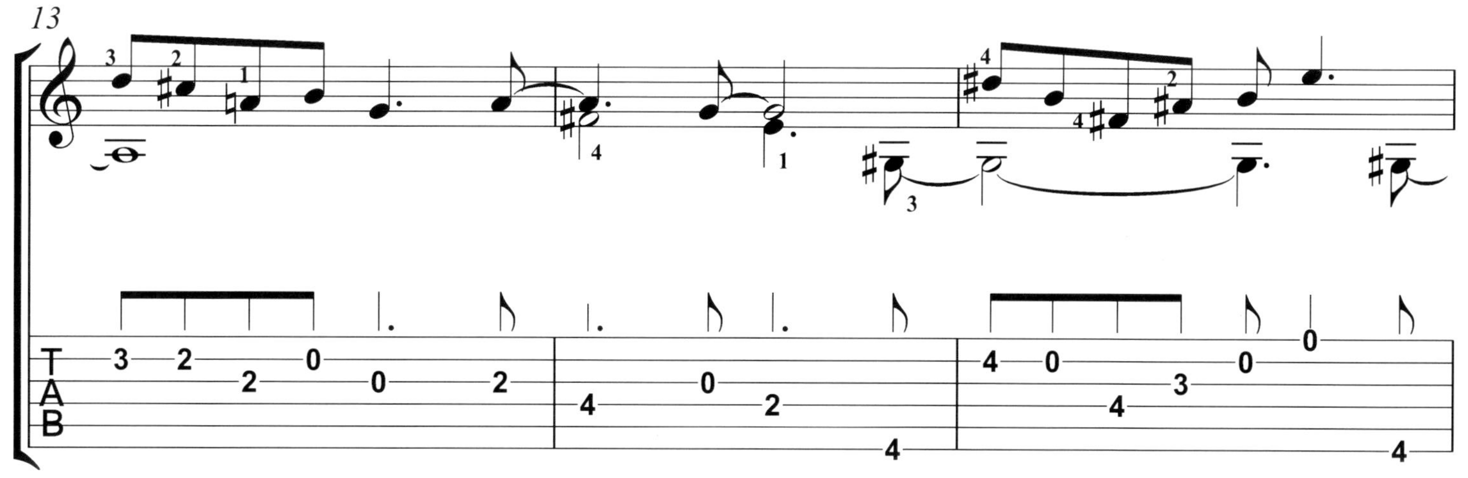

D.C. al Coda

Coda

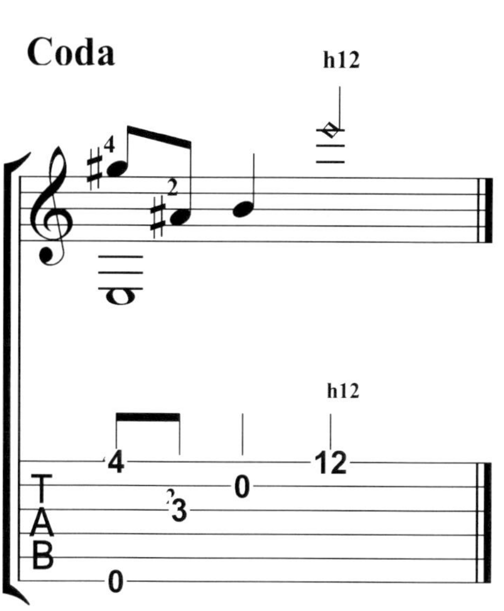

Raga #2

Gilbert Isbin

A tempo
13
1.
2.
17
h12
h12
h12
h12

What If?

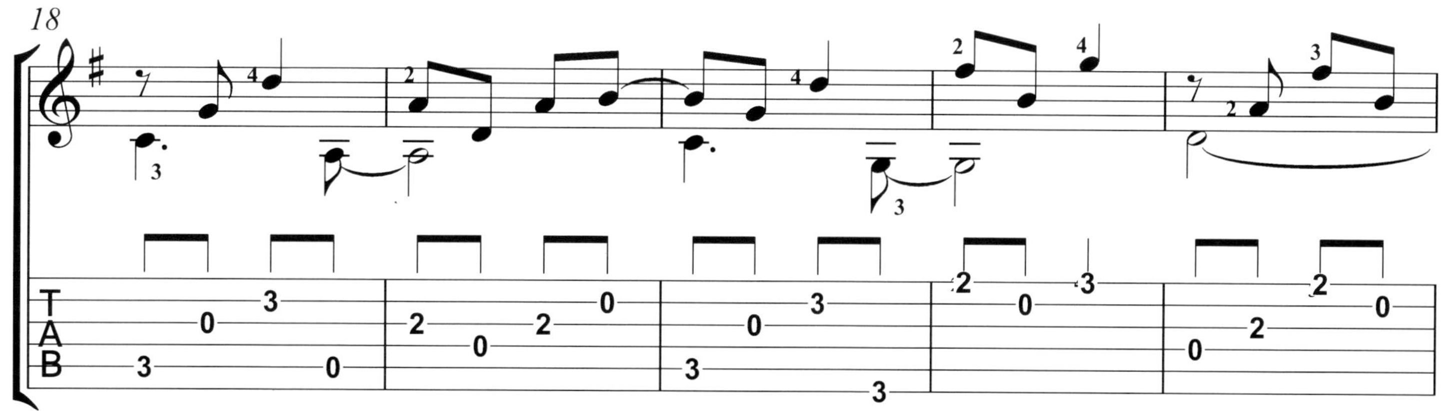

18
T
A
B

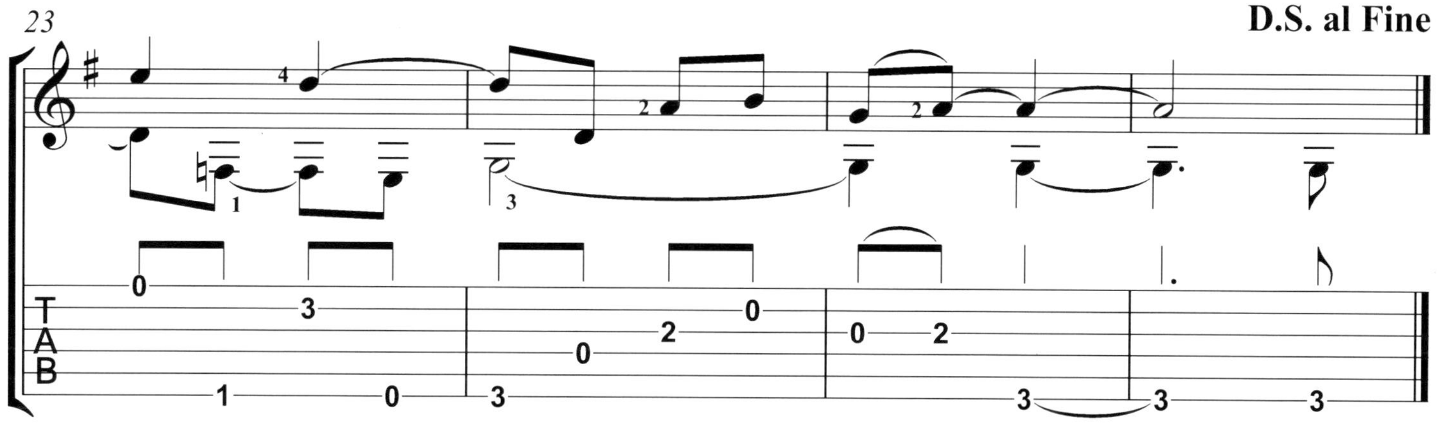

23
D.S. al Fine
T
A
B

Soon

Gilbert Isbin

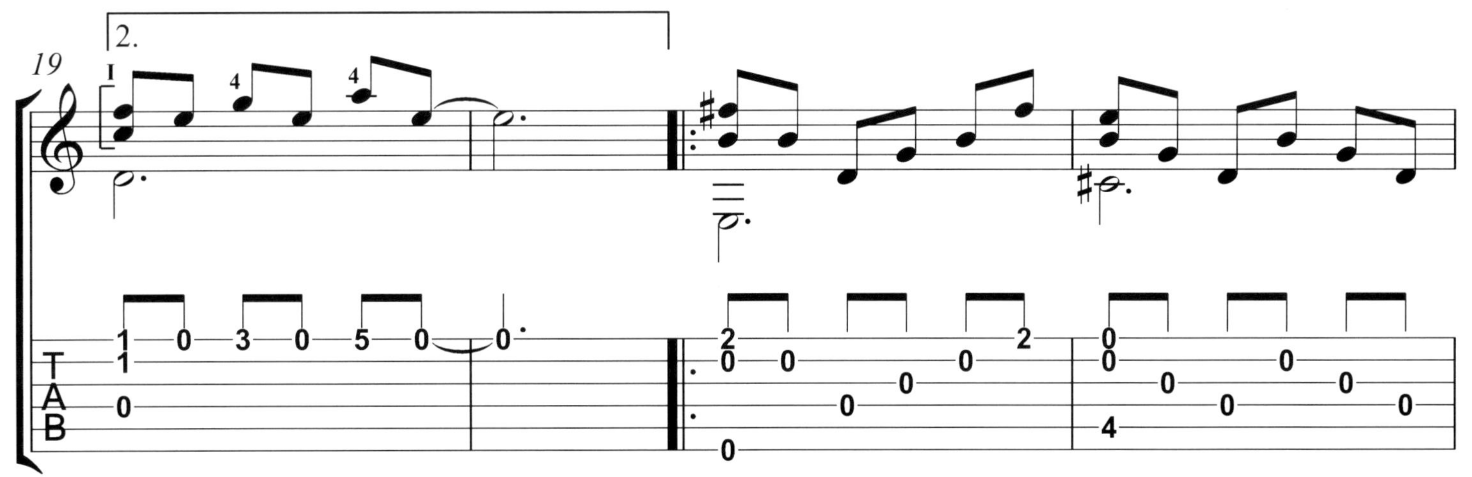
19
2.
T
A
B

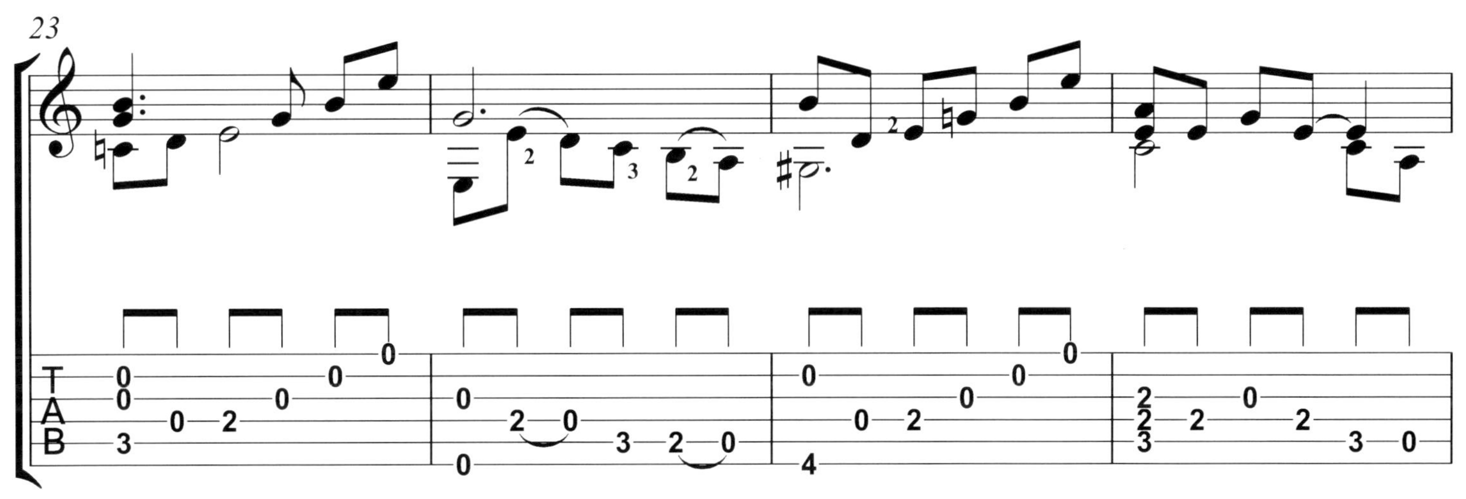
23
T
A
B

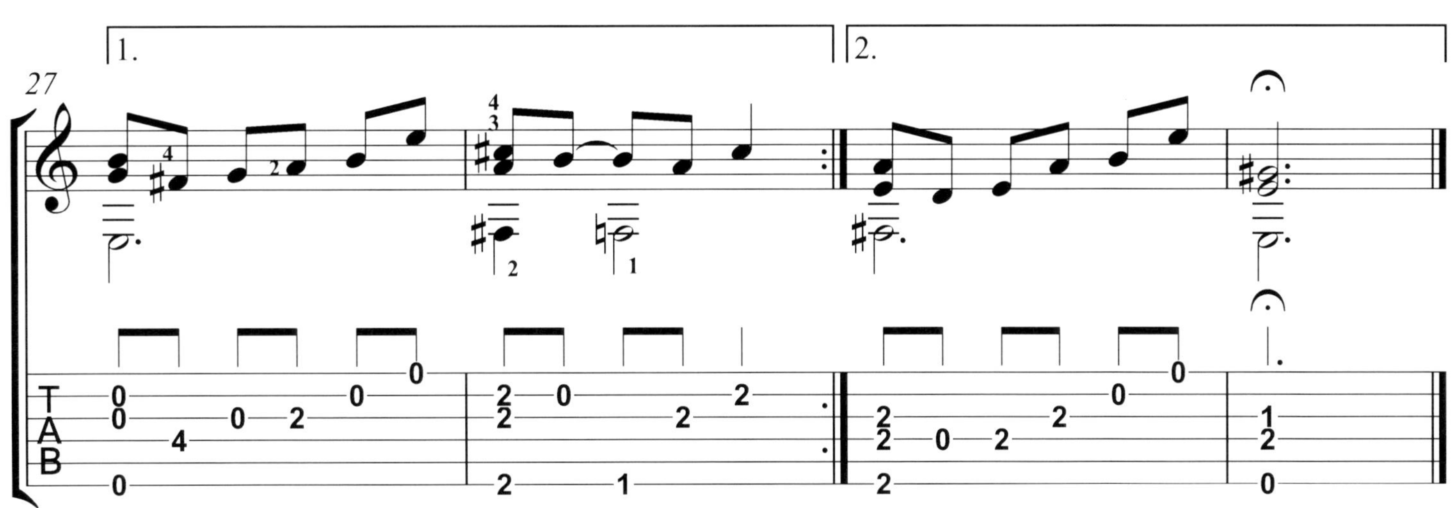
27
1.
2.
T
A
B

A Feel Good Song

28

Gilbert Isbin

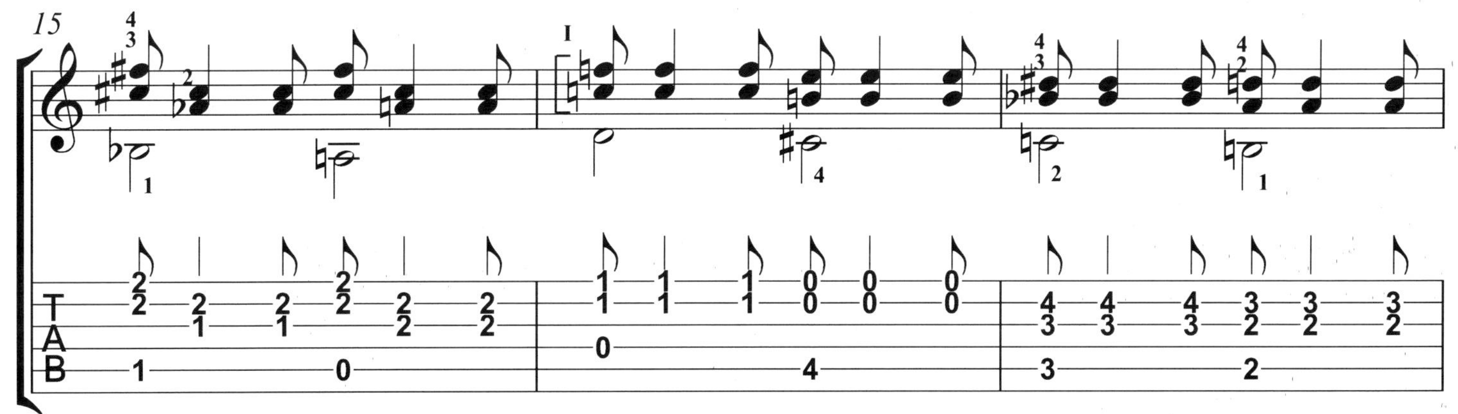
15
T
A
B

D.C. al Fine
18
T
A
B

Homecoming

♩ = 100

Gilbert Isbin

13
16
p

Let Beauty Abound

Gilbert Isbin

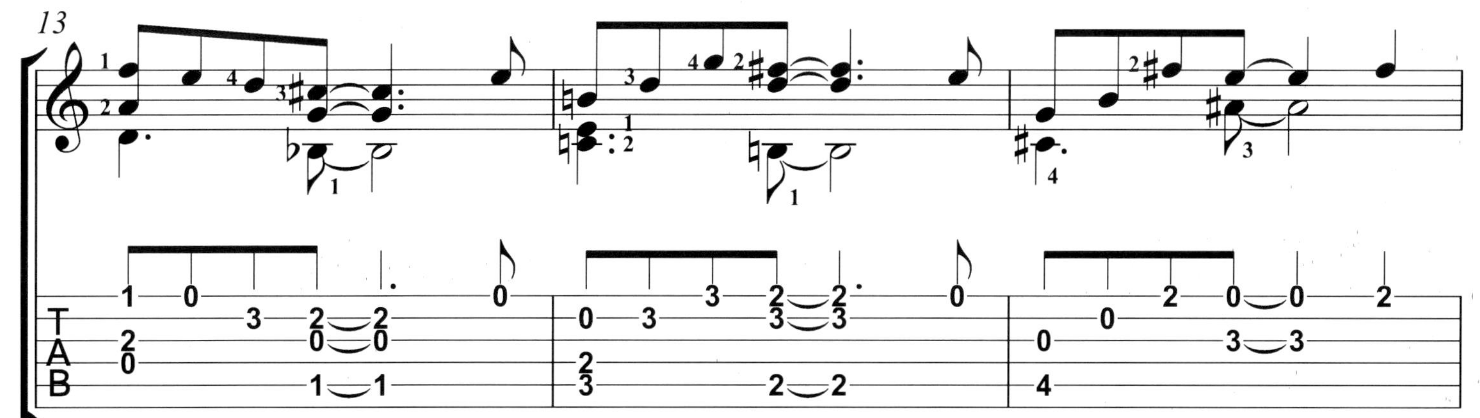
13

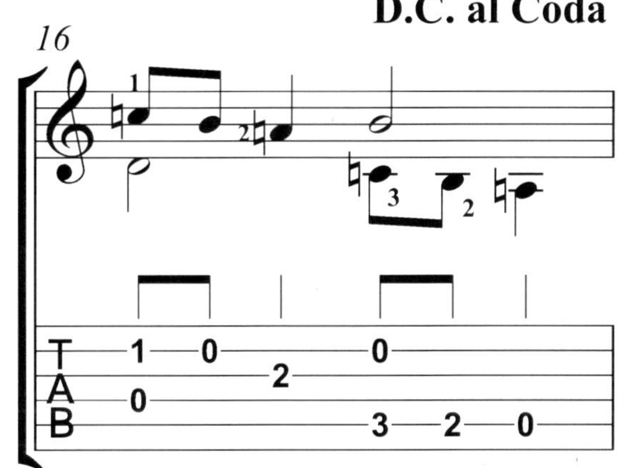
16
D.C. al Coda

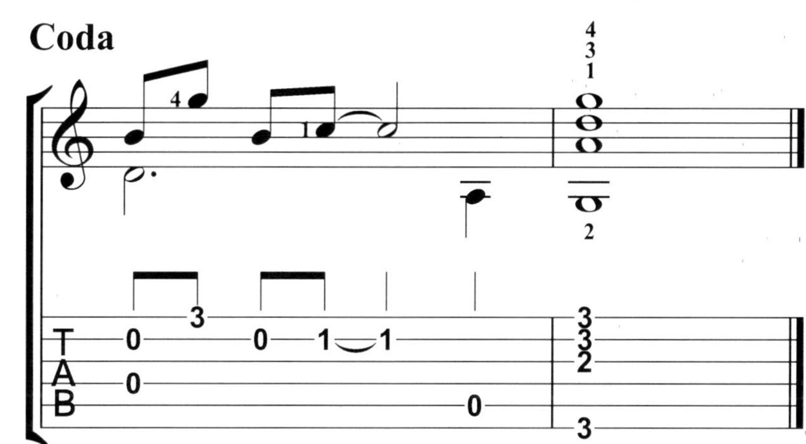
Coda

Over There

D.C. al Coda
Coda

Pale Glow

That Feels Right

Gilbert Isbin

This Moment

rit.

Slow Dance

Gilbert Isbin

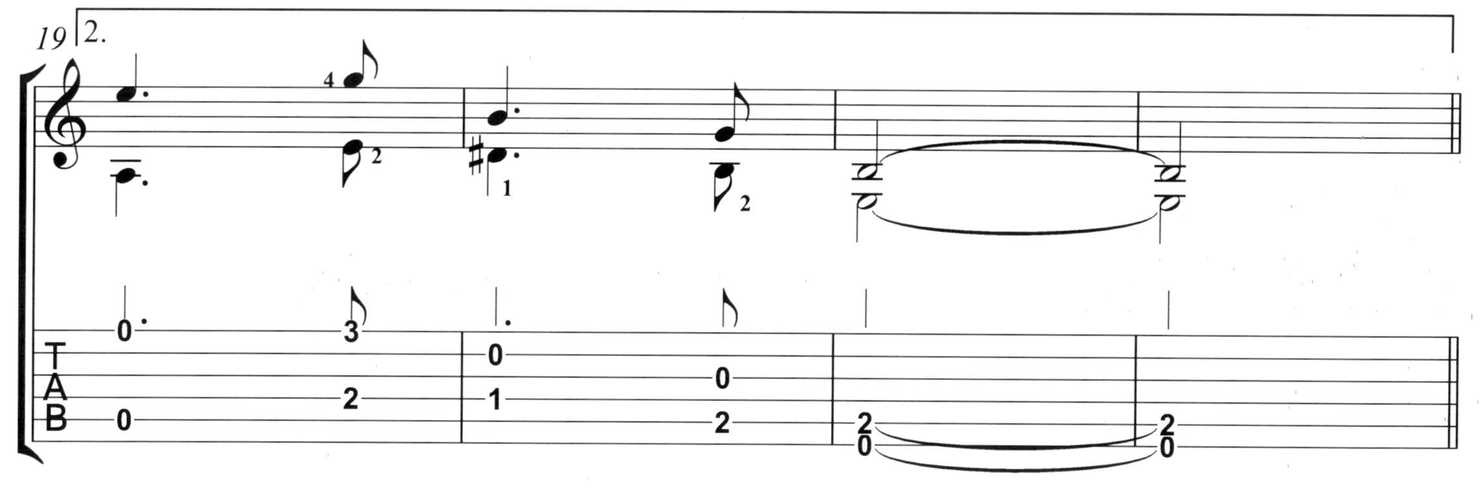
19
2.
T
A
B

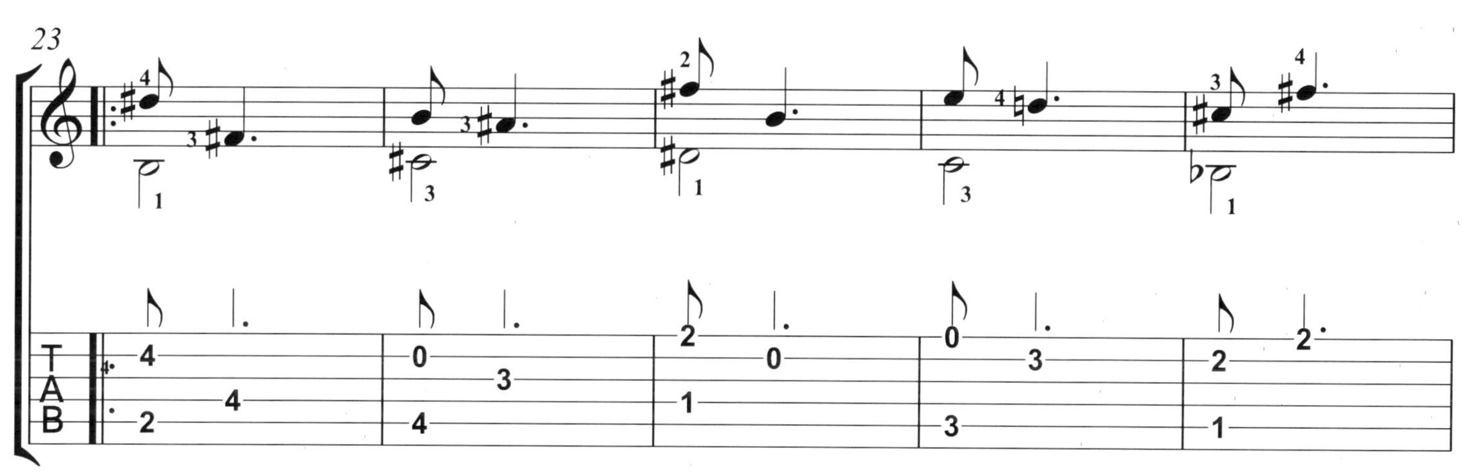
23
T
A
B

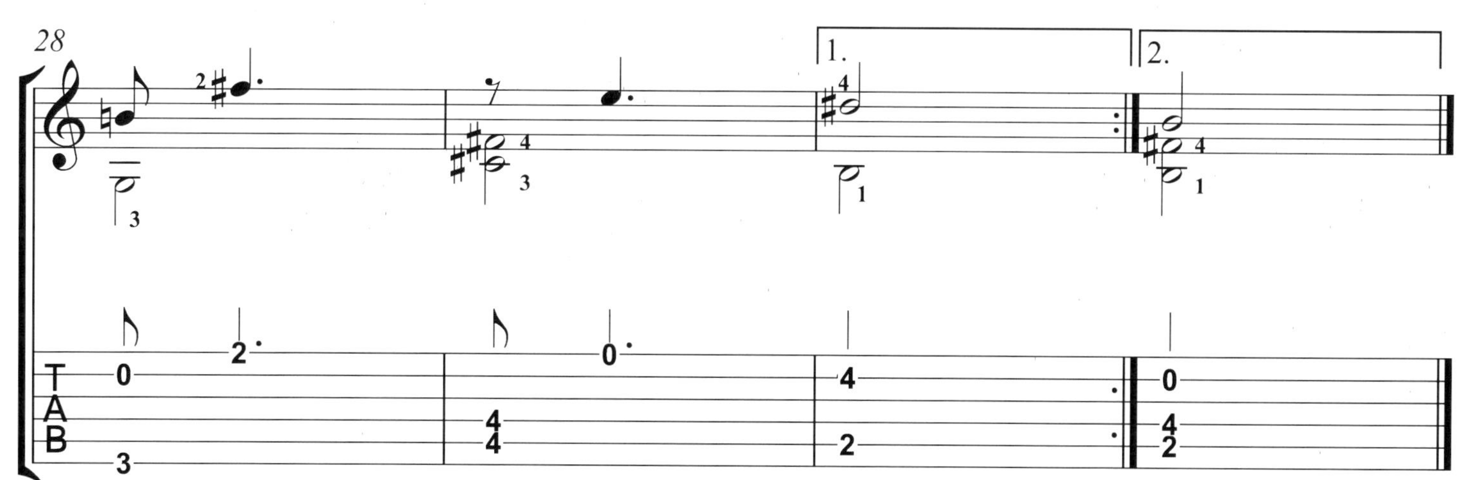
28
1.
2.
T
A
B

You've Got Me Dreaming

♩ = 60

Gilbert Isbin

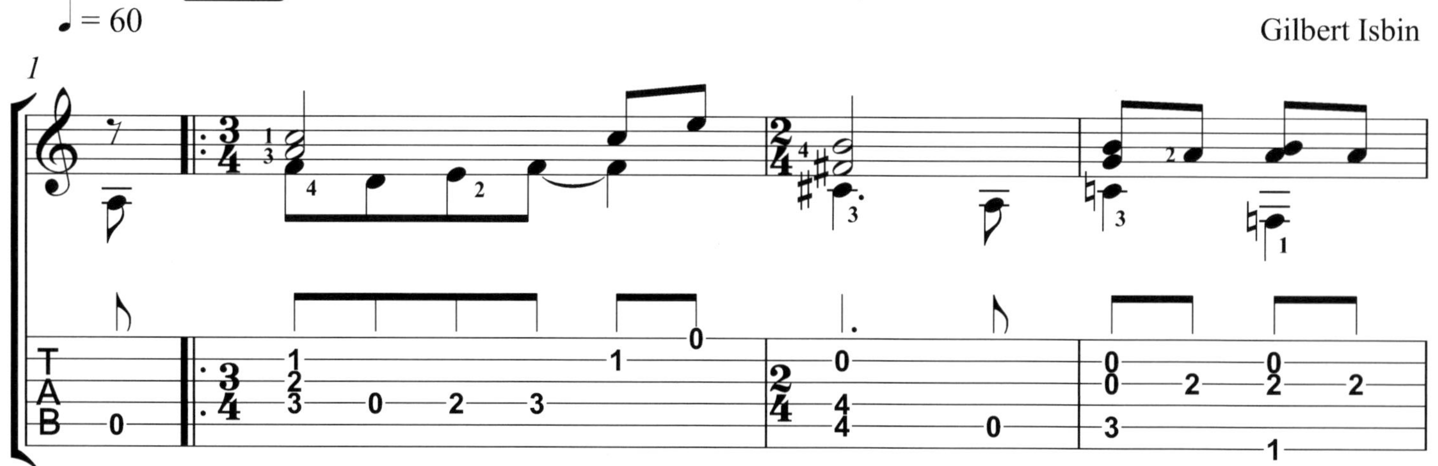

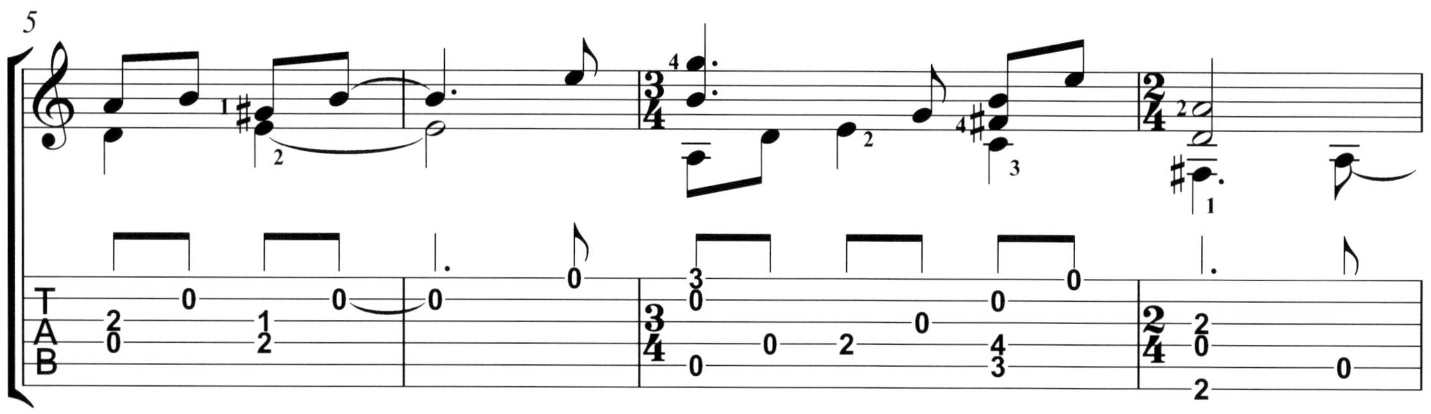

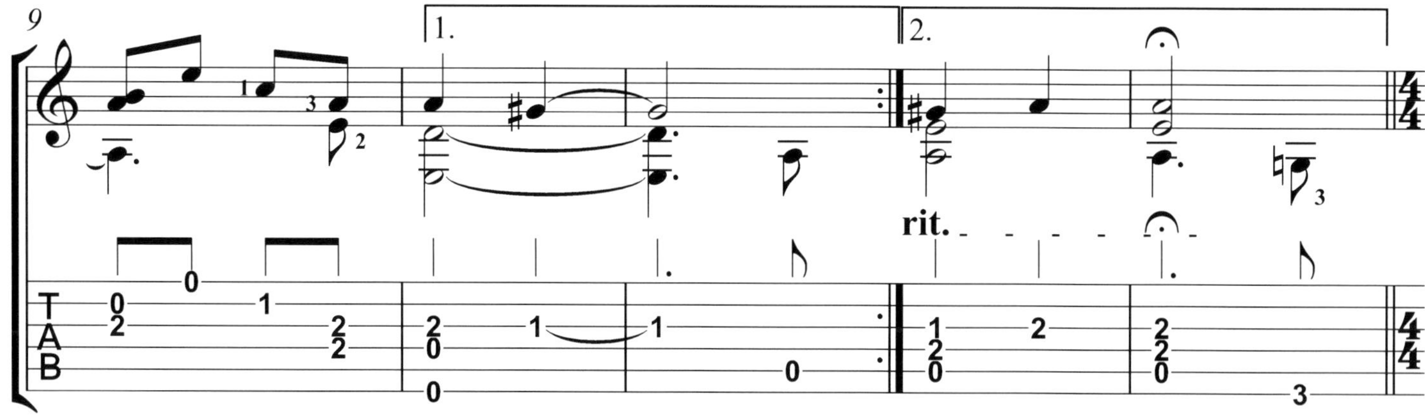

A tempo

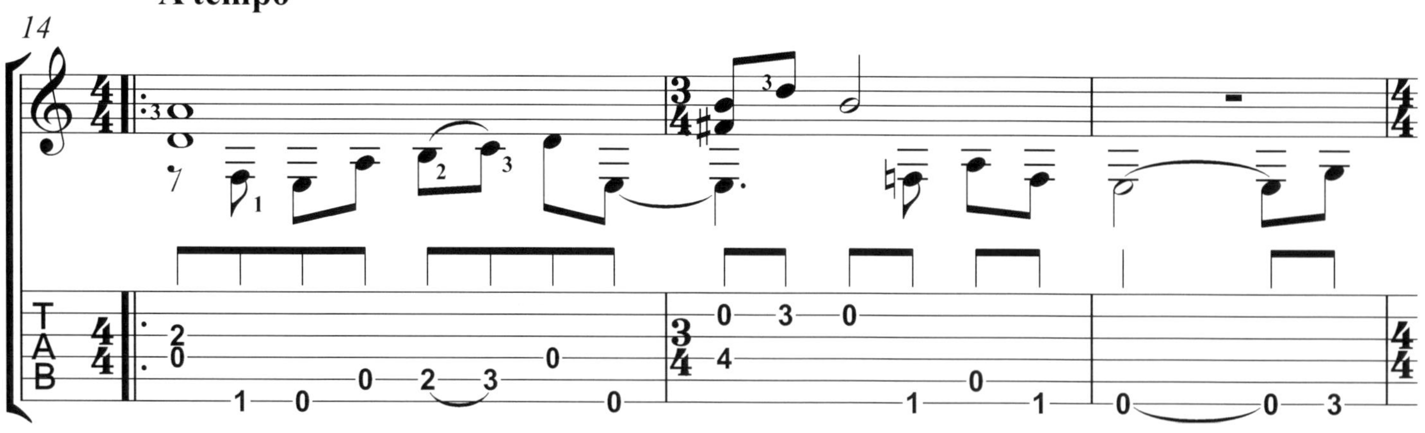

Willow Song

Gilbert Isbin

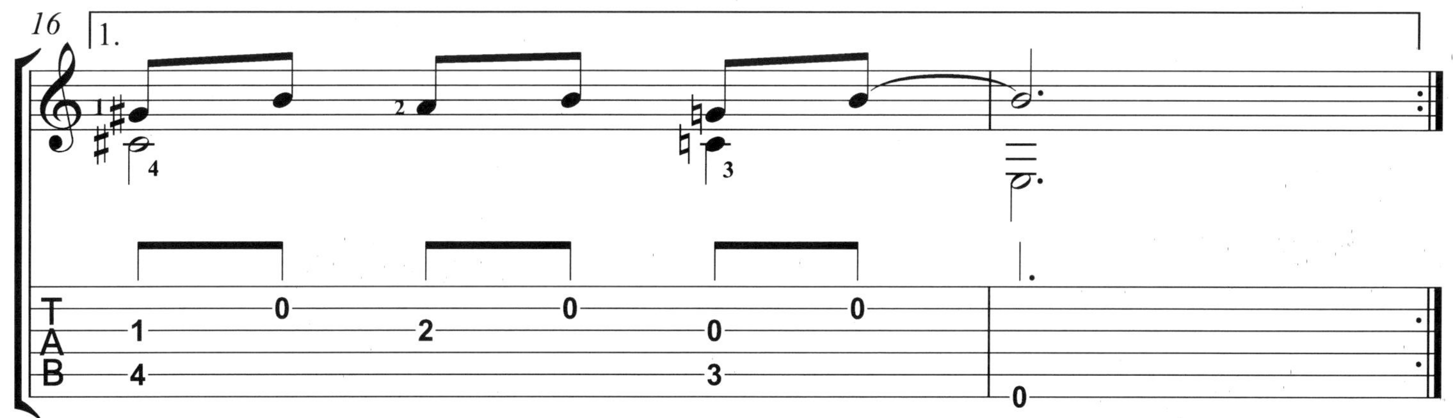

D.C. al Fine

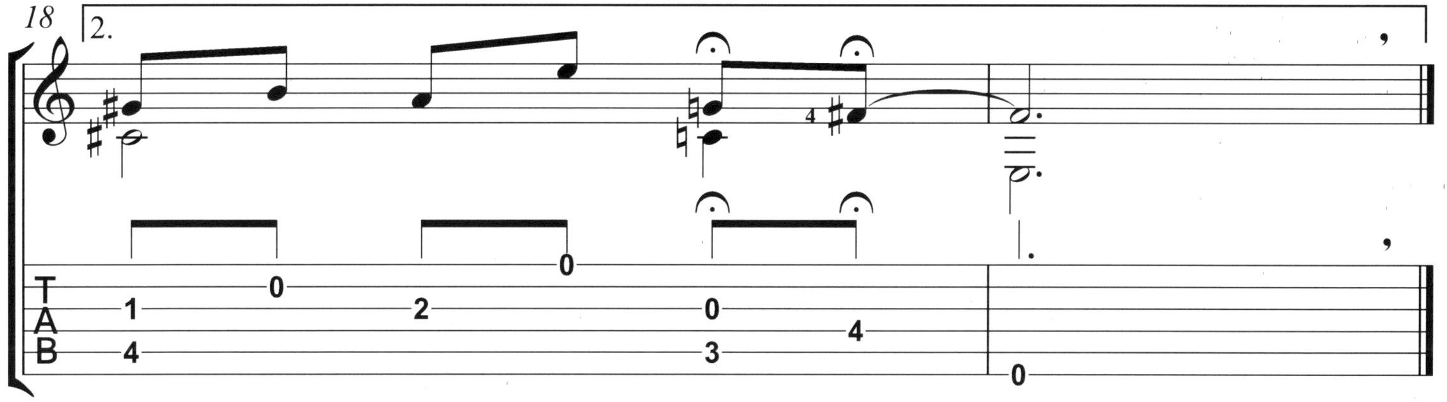

By Moonlight

Gilbert Isbin

Sunshine

39

Gilbert Isbin

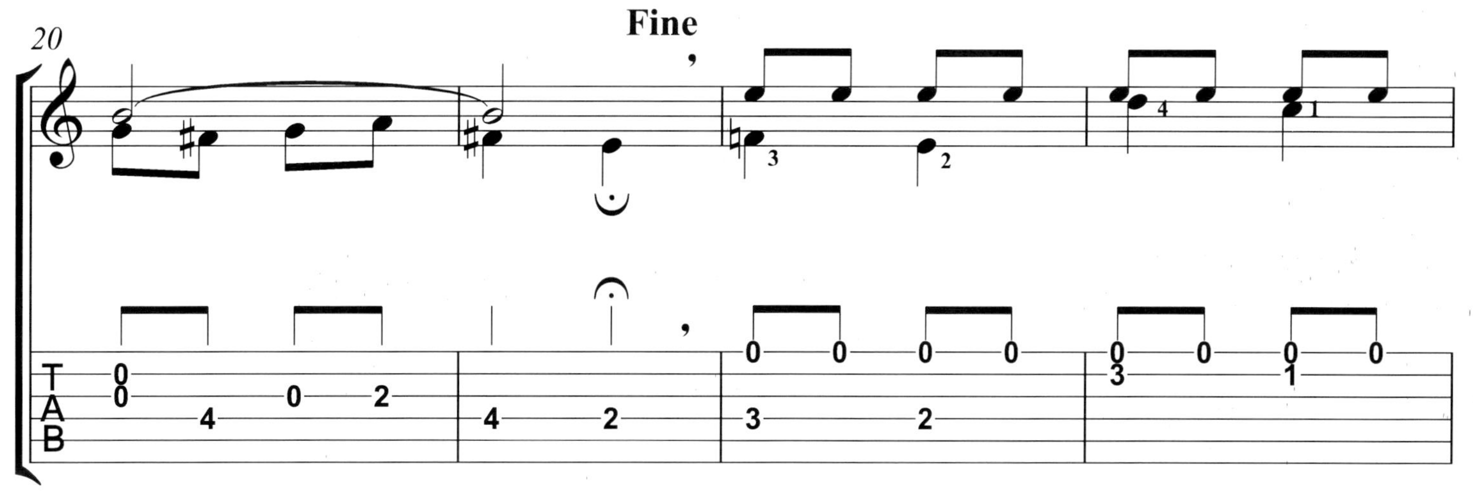
20
Fine
T
A
B

24
T
A
B

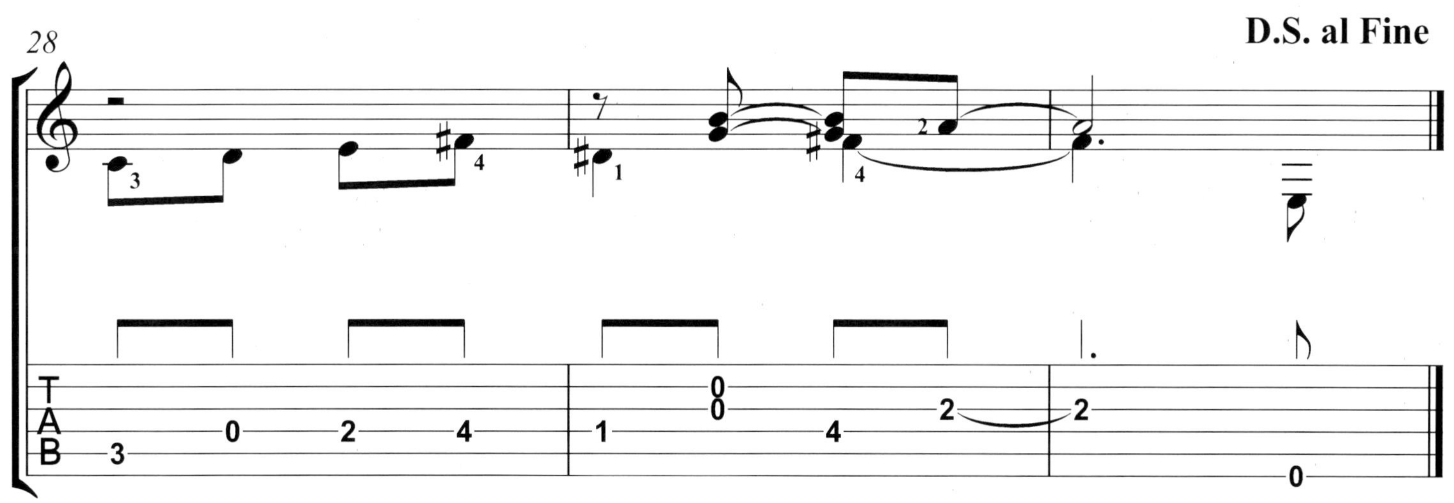
28
D.S. al Fine
T
A
B

A Quartal Experience

Gilbert Isbin

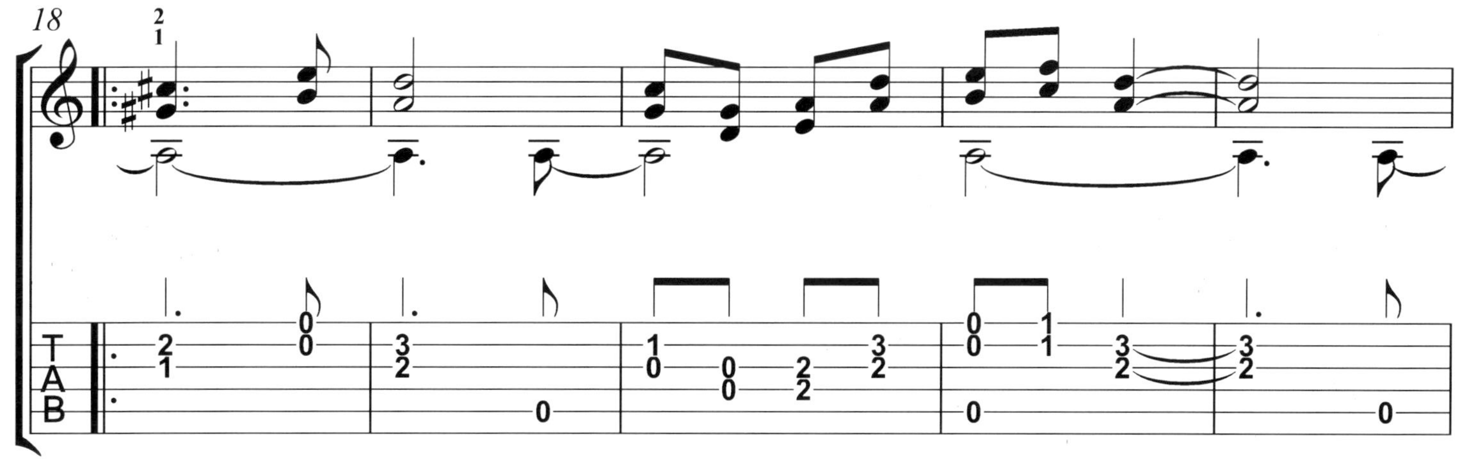

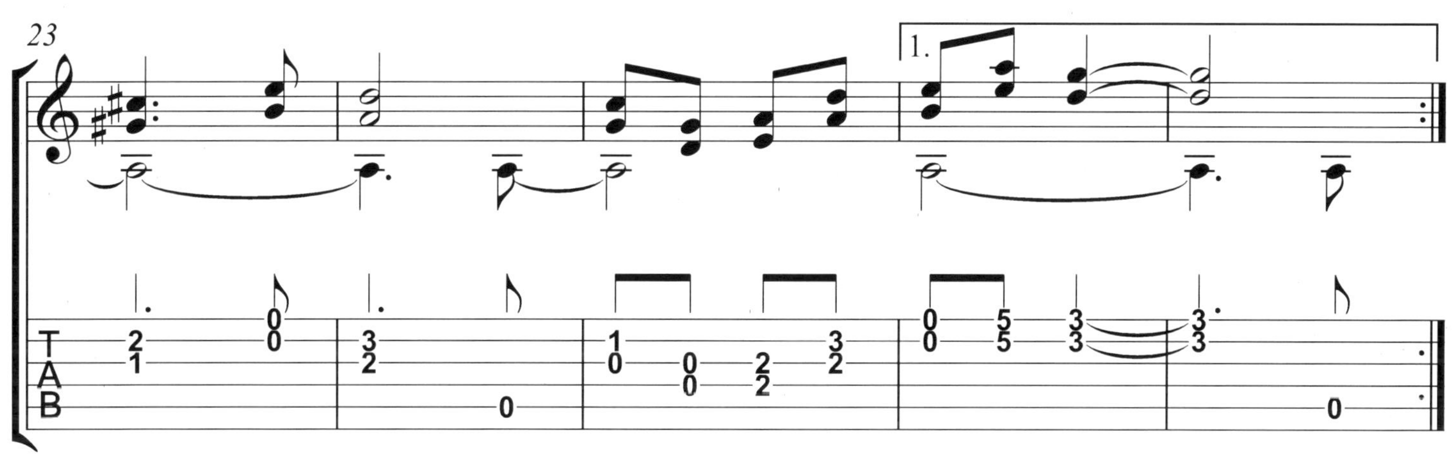

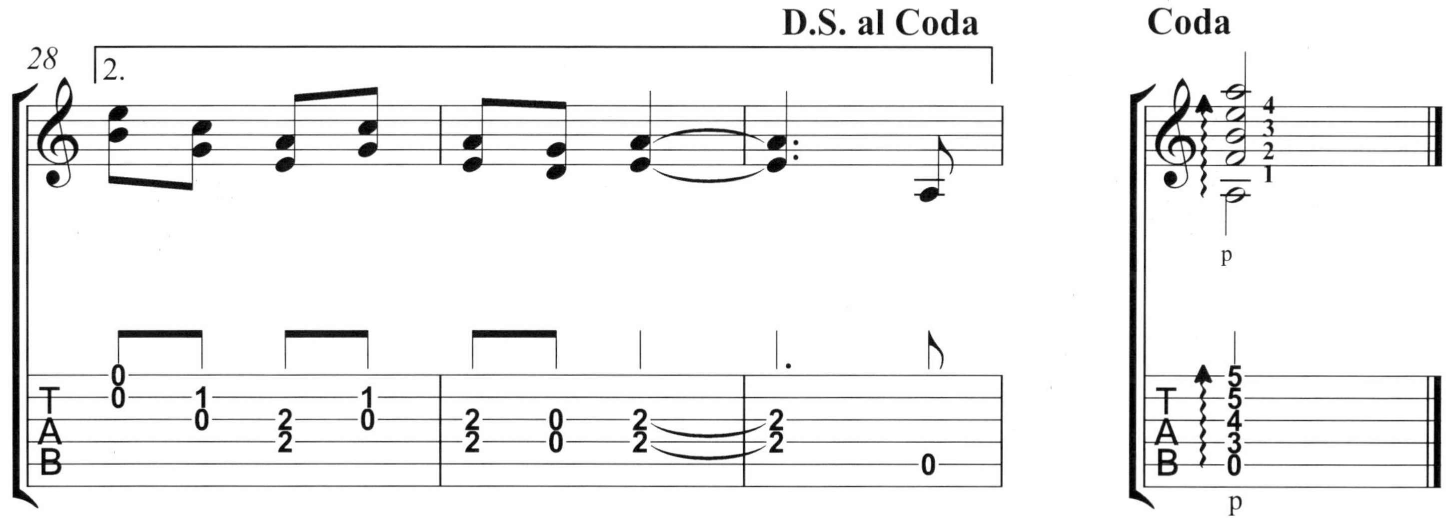
D.S. al Coda
Coda

Yearning Heart Blues

Gilbert Isbin

17
1.
T
A
B
D.C. al Fine
20
2.

A Triad Piece

42

♩ = 60

Gilbert Isbin

1.
2.
h12
h12

Thinking of You

♩ = 80

Gilbert Isbin

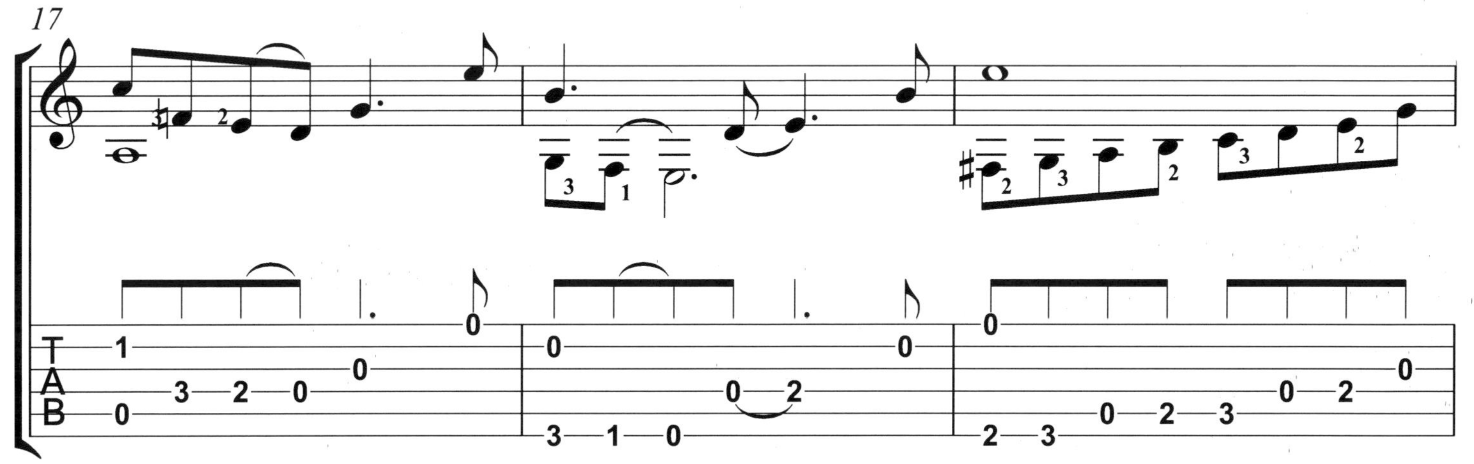
17
T
A
B

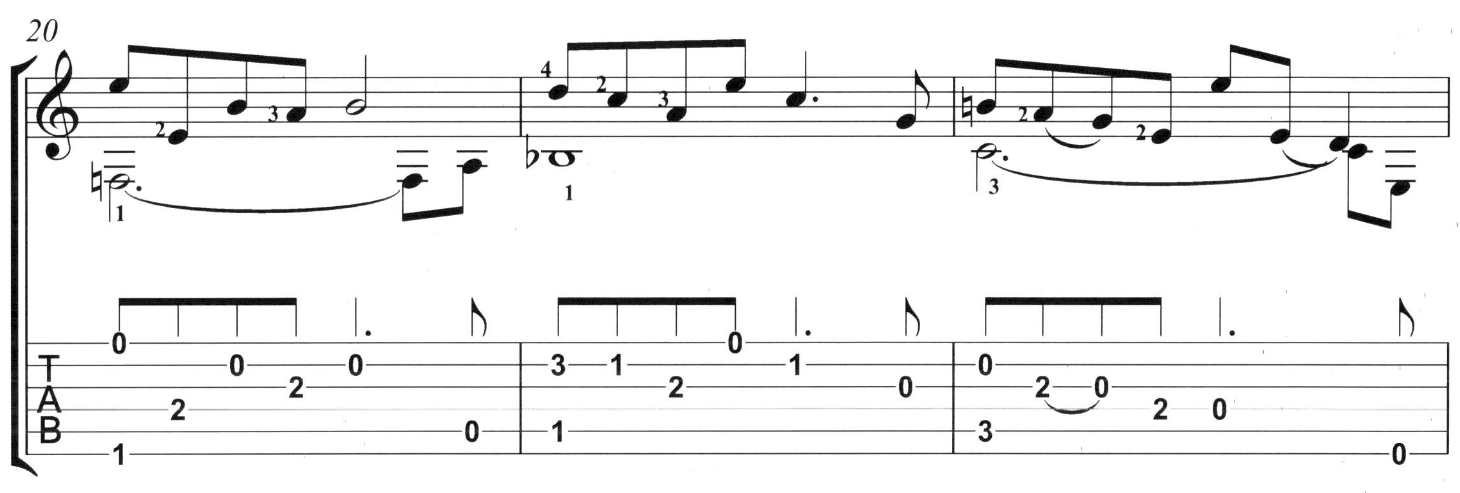
20
T
A
B

rit.
23
p
T
A
B

A Blue Song

Lento

Gilbert Isbin

rit.
D.C. al Fine

To Be Here

Gilbert Isbin

2.
13
15
rit.

A Winter's Tale

Gilbert Isbin

rit.
A tempo
molto rit.

A Fresh Beginning

Gilbert Isbin

D.C. al Coda

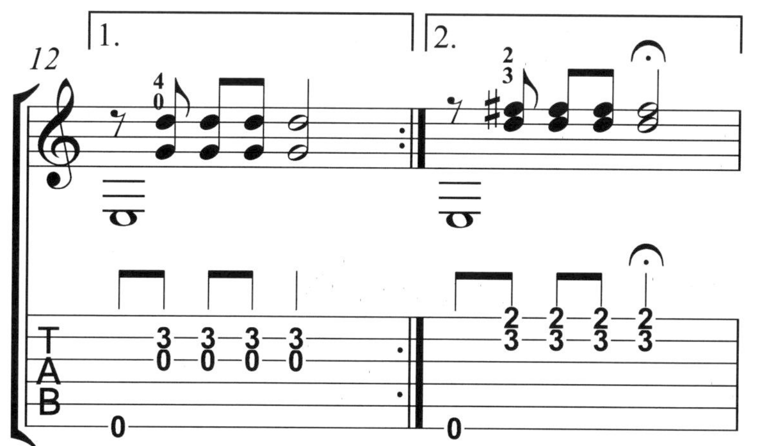

Coda

In Night's Embrace

Gilbert Isbin

1.
2.
21
25
30
34
T
A
B

Oh Tell Me

A tempo
19
23
rit.

Isn't That Peculiar?

Gilbert Isbin

To Coda
D.C. al Coda
Coda
h12

Other Mel Bay Fingerstyle Books

Other Mel Bay Fingerstyle Books

WWW.MELBAY.COM